I'M NOT YELLING I'M A DISPATCHER THAT'S HOW WE TALK

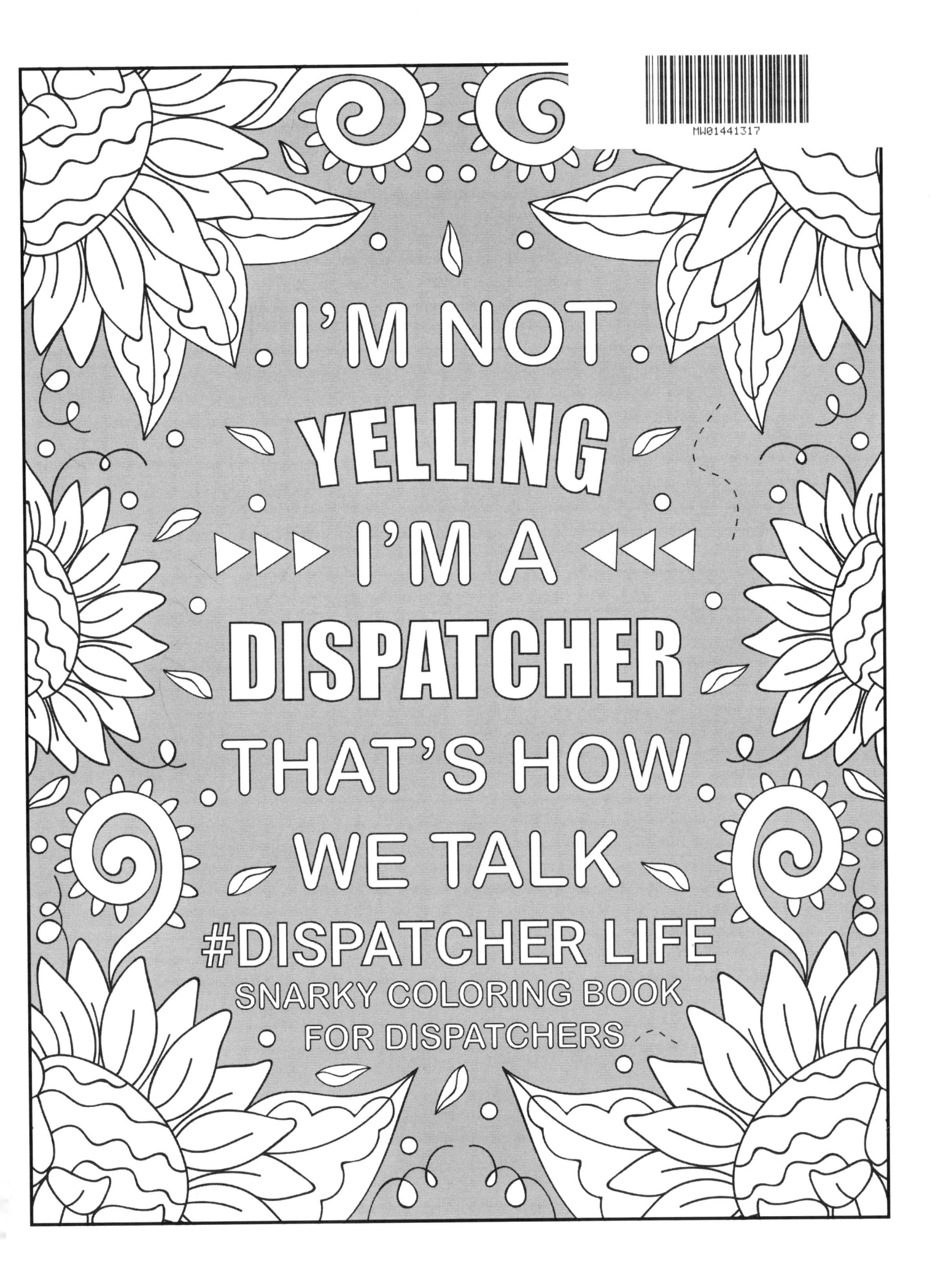

#DISPATCHER LIFE
SNARKY COLORING BOOK FOR DISPATCHERS

COLOR TEST PAGE

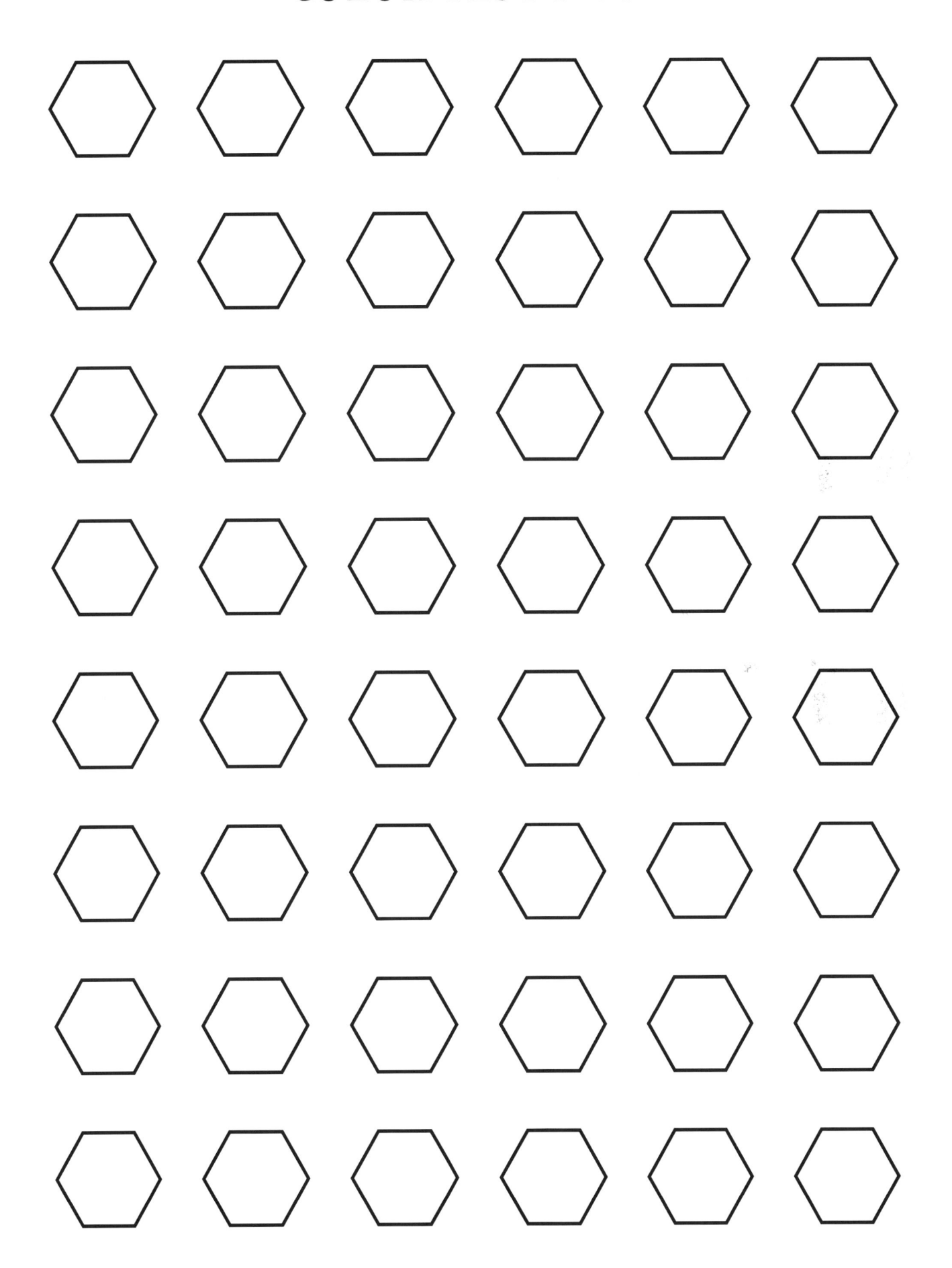

DISPATCHER
THE FIRST PERSON YOU CALL AFTER SAYING HOLD MY DRINK AND WATCH THIS

DISPATCHING is a Work of Heart

TELL ME YOUR **WORST** AND I'LL SEND YOU THE **BEST**

DON'T MAKE ME USE MY DISPATCHER VOICE!

I NEVER DREAMED
I WOULD BE A SUPER COOL
DISPATCHER
BUT HERE I AM
KILLING IT!

WORLD'S BEST DISPATCHER

I'M NOT YELLING I'M A DISPATCHER THAT'S HOW WE TALK

DISPATCHER LLAMA

AIN'T GOT TIME FOR YOUR DRAMA

NOTHING *suprises* ME ANYMORE *I am a* Dispatcher

I CAN'T FIX STUPID BUT I CAN FIX WHAT STUPID DOES

INSTANT DISPATCHER JUST ADD coffee

DISPATCHER
NUTRITION FACTS

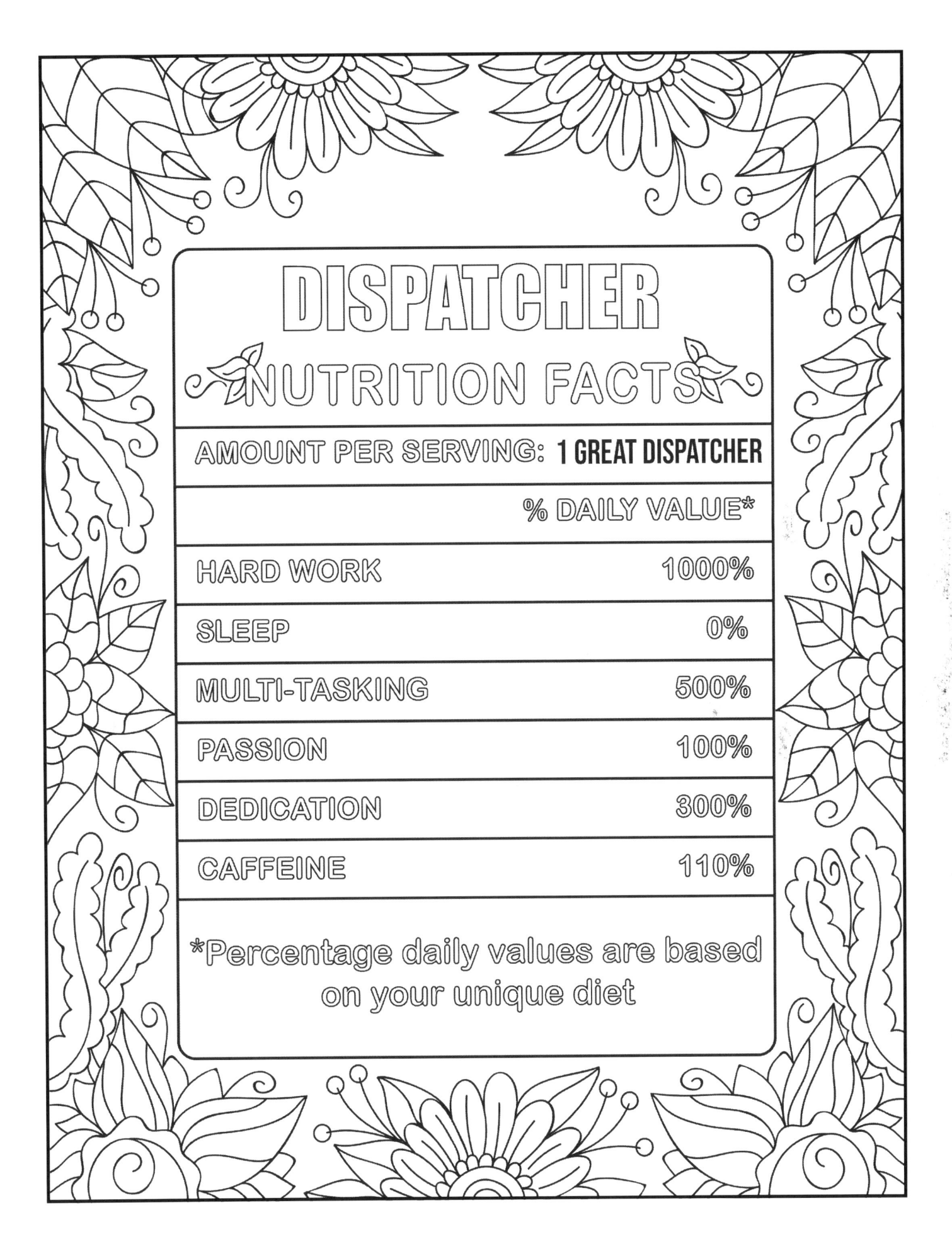

AMOUNT PER SERVING: 1 GREAT DISPATCHER

	% DAILY VALUE*
HARD WORK	1000%
SLEEP	0%
MULTI-TASKING	500%
PASSION	100%
DEDICATION	300%
CAFFEINE	110%

*Percentage daily values are based on your unique diet

DISPATCHERS DO IT ON THE RADIO

OTHER DISPATCHERS | ME

I am NOT ignoring you
I am a
DISPATCHER
and I
CAN'T hear crap
ANYMORE

BEING A DISPATCHER

Is easy...it's like

RIDING A BIKE

Except the bike is on fire

You're on fire

Everything is on fire

Dispatcher BECAUSE FABULOUS *Miracle Worker* ISN'T AN *Official Job* TITLE

STUPID PEOPLE *Keep me employed*

911 Dispatcher
MY BRAIN IS 90% POLICE CODE

911 IS MY WORK Number

DISPATCHER LIFE

I MAKE IT LOOK EASY

EVERYBODY RELAX THE DISPATCHER IS HERE THE DAY WILL BE SAVED SHORTLY

I'M A DISPATCHER. TO SAVE TIME LET'S JUST ASSUME I'M ALWAYS RIGHT

I USED TO HAVE A LIFE BUT I DECIDED TO BE A DISPATCHER